THE
Archive Photographs
SERIES
AROUND
LLANDRINDOD WELLS

THE
Archive Photographs
SERIES

AROUND
LLANDRINDOD WELLS

Compiled by
Chris Wilson

CHALFORD

In association with
Radnorshire Museum

First published 1995
Copyright © Chris Wilson, 1995

The Chalford Publishing Company
St Mary's Mill, Chalford,
Stroud, Gloucestershire, GL6 8NX

ISBN 0 7524 0191 2

Typesetting and origination by
The Chalford Publishing Company
Printed in Great Britain by
Redwood Books, Trowbridge

Cover picture: Group outside Metropole Hotel, *c.* 1900.

Contents

Introduction

Although the existence of the springs at Llandrindod Wells had been known for centuries, the first proven attempt to take commercial advantage was not until 1732 when a Mrs Jenkins began to sell the waters to travellers, as a result of which, their fame began to spread. Her farm became known as the Pump House, the forerunner of the famous Pump House Hotel, now the site of Powys County Hall.

The springs were situated on a bleak common, the first sight of which dismayed many visitors, who expected 'a fine village, with terraces of fine lodging houses, and nice walks in front for the ladies and their beaux to walk upon, and lots of fine looking shops, where everything eatable and wearable could be purchased, with a "Grand Hotel" in the centre'. Accommodation at this time, however, was provided at farmhouses spread around the common, or at the Llanerch Inn, and facilities were rather primitive.

In 1749 William Grosvenor of Shrewsbury, a man described as being of 'enterprising spirit' converted Llandrindod Hall, a deserted farmhouse, into a splendid hotel described as having 'accommodation for the invalid of whatever rank and distinction, field amusements for the healthy, while balls, billiards and regular assemblies varied the pastimes of the gay and fashionable. The grounds were not only ornamented in a style of elegance, but on them were discernable the finished suggestions of the most polished taste. There were fishponds, always well stocked, and what may now appear incredible, swans of varied plumes gracing their surface.'

In 1756 Dr Diederick Wessel Linden, an eminent German physician, published *A Treatise on the Three Medicinal Mineral Waters at Llandrindod*. This work brought the 'healing properties' of the wells to the attention of a wider public. It was this work more than anything which was to secure the immediate future success of the spa. Linden had come to the wells himself to receive treatment for the effects of years spent testing mineral springs and for 'an inveterate scurvy; which had for several years soured my juices and irritated them on every occasion'. He described how after taking the waters for some four weeks he was 'cured, to my own unspeakable comfort, and the great surprise of all my friends and acquaintances'.

For thirty years the area flourished as a resort for the healthy and infirm alike, but like many inland spas a period of decline resulted from the advent of sea bathing as a fashionable cure. The first hotel of William Grosvenor, meanwhile, burned down before the end of the eighteenth century (a farm stands in its place today).

Although visitors continued to frequent the wells during the early years of the nineteenth century, development on a large scale was inhibited by the remoteness of the area and the lack of good building land. The turning point came with the enclosure of the common in 1862, which enabled building work, and the construction of the railway.

The first section of the Central Wales line from Knighton to Llandrindod was opened in 1865 and the whole line was completed in 1868, giving a through connection from Shrewsbury to Swansea. Llandrindod was now within easy reach for the people living in the large industrial towns and cities of the North West of England, the Midlands and South Wales. The easing of transport difficulties heralded the start of a boom in the town's popularity. Visitors began to come in large numbers as for the first time the 'holiday' was no longer the sole preserve of the wealthy.

A new spring was discovered in 1867 and a pump room and bath-house were soon erected, gardens were laid out and the whole area became known as the Rock Park.

The land around the Rock Park saw rapid development forming the centre of a new and expanding town. By the early 1870s the surrounding land had been filled with new streets, a Market Hall, the Congregational Church, shops, hotels and private houses. Progress was slower on the land to the east of the railway. The Holy Trinity Church was built in 1871 and some private houses and a hotel along the main road, Temple Street. In the early 1870s the marshy land near the Pump House Hotel was drained to form an ornamental lake. Llandrindod Wells was now beginning to take shape as a town designed to meet the varied needs of Victorian visitors.

Between 1865 and 1914 the appearance was that of a boom town. Hotels and boarding houses sprang up along the new streets and shops were opened to meet the needs of visitors and residents alike. Many private houses were built on the grand scale characteristic of the time.

In the early 1880s Middleton Street had consisted of wooden shanties and open air stalls, but it gradually replaced High Street as the focal point of the town. The most famous shop was probably the Central Wales Emporium, opened on the corner of Temple Street and Station Crescent in 1881 by William Thomas of Penybont. It sold a large variety of goods, including a range of illustrated guide books and a type of cloth named 'spa flannel'. This business closed in 1927, by which time the spa and the town was in decline.

The season at Llandrindod traditionally lasted from May until mid-September. Outside the pump rooms at the Rock Park and Pump House Hotel visitors queued each morning to take the waters, entertained by music from orchestras. The amount drunk varied from two to six glasses at a time, depending on the type of ailment, the effects of which, judging from letters and journals were quite startling. A journal of 1774 tells the following tale: 'An old man who lives near the spring, and from whom I had this account, told me that he was ill for several years and so windy and costive that his life was a burden to him. He applied to several apothecaries and physicians who gave him no relief. He at last took to the waters of which he drunk 23 pints which brought from him an excrement so hard as he could make little or no impression on when stamped with the heel of a shoe! This man is upwards of 70 years old and has drank the water frequently after and hath never had a sick day since that time and looks though very grey the most healthy man I have seen of his age'.

The charge at both pump rooms was 6d per day for any amount of water. In 1909 the High Street Baths opened, offering the wide range of electrical treatments which were expected at a modern spa.

The spacious lay out of the town meant that it could cater for the growing popularity of outdoor sports. A private nine hole golf course, possibly the first in Wales, was opened on the common by the Pump House Hotel in 1893. The 18 hole course above the lake opened as a club in 1906. Many of the larger hotels had tennis courts and croquet lawns on their grounds and horse races and later air displays were held on the Rock Ddole, a meadow near the river.

During the First World War the town became home for refugees and wounded soldiers. Hotels and boarding houses were taken over as billets for soldiers on training courses. The poor economic situation during the depression of the 1920s and 1930s led to several bad years for the town during which many hotels and boarding houses were turned into private homes and flats. The Second World War again saw the town as a centre for military hospitals and billets. Lean years following the war again led to hardship for the town and only the large hotels were able to survive into the present.

To the south of Llandrindod Wells are the villages of Newbridge-on-Wye, Disserth and Howey. Newbridge, built on the banks of the Wye, was probably a traditional crossing place from as far back as the Roman occupation. The town grew in importance, however, as a stopping-off point on the drovers' route between Tregaron and the English cattle markets. During the last century there were as many as thirteen public houses in the village to cater for travellers. The now demolished Sun Inn was a safe house for rioters during the Rebecca Riots of 1843-44.

The small hamlet of Disserth lies half way between Newbridge and Howey and was another stop-over for the drovers. Howey, Llandrindod's nearest neighbour, was for many years the postal address for any mail coming to Llandrindod. Other villages, within a few miles of Llandrindod, and also included in this volume are Llanyre, Crossgates and Penybont.

Acknowledgements

The photographs in this volume come principally from the collections of the Radnorshire Museum. We acknowledge a great debt of thanks to all those generous people who in the past, present and, we hope, the future have donated and will continue to donate their photographs and postcards to the museum, together with information about their content. Thanks must also go to Powys Archives for the loan of images to fill some gaps in the collection and for their help and advice.

Special thanks must go to the staff of the Radnorshire Museum, Geoff Webster for his knowledge of the collection and assistance in collating the images to be used; and to Alison Duffell, June Pugh, Sarah Carter, Leah Bywater and Lynda Stephens who have over the last two years spent a great deal of time cataloguing what is a vast collection of reference material; the work's not finished yet!

Thanks must also go to Eva Bredsdorff for her help on the proofs. Finally I would like to thank Richard Meredith for making available to us both his expertise and collections.

One
Views of
Llandrindod Wells

Llandrindod Wells from the hills overlooking the Lake. The boathouse and café can be seen on the lakeside with the Pump House Hotel and Pump Room on the right of the picture. The photograph is attributed to Villiers.

A second photograph attributed to Villiers showing Llandrindod Wells from the common. This more than any other view highlights the bleakness of the landscape surrounding the town during the early years of its development.

The Lake, boathouse and café with the Pump House Hotel in the background. The Lake had been created out of marshy ground in the early 1870s and by 1909 was municipally owned with a new boathouse and café.

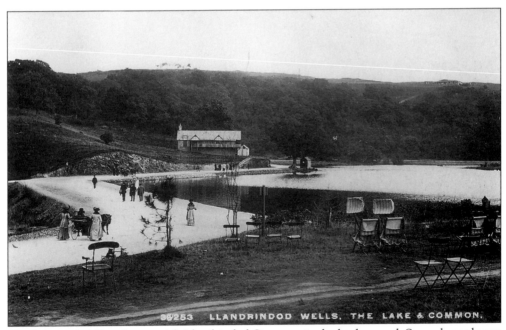

The Lake and old boathouse with Llandrindod Common in the background. Several people can be seen being taken around the Lake in pony-drawn invalid carriages.

The Lake, Llandrindod Wells. Once populated by swans, recent attempts to reintroduce them have unfortunately proved unsuccessful as the cygnets have been dying from lead shot poisoning.

Lakeside festivities, *c.* 1912. Photograph by Thomas Roberts.

The 'Shakey Bridge' over the River Ithon. The original bridge dating from the 1890s was made up of boards suspended on wires. Visitors were warned that no more than three people should attempt to cross at one time! The current safer bridge was built in 1940. The photograph is attributed to Villiers.

The 'Alpine Bridge' on the Ithon. The photograph is attributed to Villiers.

'Lovers Leap', the Rock Park, a popular local beauty spot with the early visitors to the spa. The River Ithon below, however, contains dangerous currents and many have lost their lives in its waters. The photograph is attributed to Villiers.

This early photograph of the Rock Park shows the Chalybeate Spring in the foreground. The photograph dates from before 1872 when the grounds began to be laid out as an arboretum. It also shows the original pump room and bathhouse erected in 1867.

Villiers' photograph of the Rock Park, with Park Terrace, the Congregational Chapel and the Gwalia Hotel in the background. By about 1900 the grounds of the Park were already well established.

This view of the Rock Park is the only one in the County Council's possession which shows the old stone bridge – recently redeveloped – within the park. The photograph is attributed to Villiers.

The Pump Room, Rock Park. New springs were discovered in 1893 and a new pump room and baths were quickly developed to provide the many new treatments on offer to the visitor. Here visitors can be seen being entertained by one of the many troupes which performed at the park. The photograph is attributed to Villiers.

Two
Street Scenes

Llandrindod High Street, looking towards Rock Park, *c.* 1870. The earliest street view in the collection, it predates the building of the Market Hall in 1872. The building in the foreground is the town's first post office built in 1869.

Park Terrace. Work began on this street overlooking the Rock Park in 1874. This view towards the 'old' Gwalia on the corner of High Street remains little changed today. The photograph is attributed to Villiers.

Park Terrace. Looking the opposite way to the previous photograph. This view concentrates on Cadwallader House which in 1896 became the town's new Post Office and Savings Bank. Photograph attributed to Villiers.

A heavily wooded Ithon Road. One of the first streets to be built during the early stages of the town's development (1868), by 1870 a Calvinist Methodist chapel had been opened here. Photograph attributed to Villiers.

Looking up Ithon Road to Park Crescent, *c.* 1900. On the immediate right of the photograph is the Albert Hall – built in 1896 to seat nearly 700 people – next to the Calvinist Chapel with the Gwalia Hotel further up the street. Photograph attributed to Villiers.

The junction of High Street and Park Crescent. In front of the Congregational Church, carriages wait to take visitors to the golf course. The Market Hall on the left had been reopened in 1909 by Llandrindod Wells Baths Ltd to provide the latest medical treatments.

Looking north up Middleton Street, a view little changed today. Of note, further down the street on the right, is the clock tower of the Victoria Hall built in 1897 at a time when Middleton Street was beginning to rival High Street as the commercial heart of the new town. Photograph attributed to Villiers.

Plas Winton Square at the southern end of Middleton Street. Horse-driven carriages and pony-driven invalid carriages vie for space with a couple of automobiles.

Middleton Street. Looking the opposite way to the previous photograph, the Plas Winton Hotel can be seen in the background. In the foreground is the Victoria Hall, used by the Radnorshire County Council from 1898 to 1909.

South Crescent. The Brynawel Hotel, far right, overlooks the croquet lawns laid out in Temple Gardens. Next to the Brynawel is the Lansdowne Hotel, today the Conservative Club. Photograph attributed to Villiers.

South Crescent. A later view than the previous photograph, the Brynawel Hotel has been enlarged and the Kington and Radnor Bank is being constructed on the corner with Temple Street. Photograph attributed to Villiers.

South Crescent after the completion of the final stage of building. The buildings remain little changed today, though the croquet lawns and tennis courts of Temple Gardens have given way to landscaped grounds. Photograph attributed to Villiers.

Lindens Walk and Temple Gardens. Looking across from Temple Street towards Lindens Walk with the Lindens Hotel and Holy Trinity Church in the background.

24

Station Crescent, 1896. In the foreground is William Thomas's Central Wales Emporium next to Thomas Wellings, architects. In the background Victoria House can be seen on the corner of Middleton Street while the covered awnings belong to W.H. Smith. Photograph attributed to Villiers.

A later view of Station Crescent highlighting the Central Wales Emporium. This business was first established in 1799 with shops in Penybont and Howey. It was opened on the corner of Temple Street and Station Crescent by William Thomas of Penybont in 1881. Next to the Emporium, and above Bufton & Son, auctioneers, can be seen the glass roofed studio of, firstly Thomas, then Rousham and Percy Roberts, photographers. Photograph attributed to Villiers.

Church Street, now Spa Road West, prior to 1909, looking towards Holy Trinity Church. In the extreme bottom left are the notices for the site of 'Tom Norton Ltd', later the Automobile Palace Ltd. On the corner of Church Street is Bound's Dispensing Chemists. Photograph attributed to Villiers.

The junction of Temple Street and Church Street, *c.* 1909. The notice on the left on the site for 'Tom Norton Ltd' advertises 'Norton's Covered Motor Charabanc'. It goes on to list the daily services for that week. Wednesday is for Llanwrtyd Wells, every other day is for the Elan Valley. Tickets could be booked at their High Street depot from where the service departed. The notice also advertises Ariel golf clubs and balls. Photograph attributed to Villiers.

Looking north along Temple Street. On the left are shops advertising cigars and confectionery, keys and boots and a haircutting, shaving, and shampooing salon. Past the awning of Worcester House on the left are the China Tea Rooms and next door the Bridge Hotel, built in 1872. Photograph attributed to Villiers.

The Ridgebourne. Most development took place during the later years of the town's growth. The Kingsland, Caerleon, Orielton and Brampton hotels can be seen from left to right in this view. Photograph attributed to Villiers.

Three
Buildings

The Llanerch Inn. An old coaching inn, it was one of the earliest buildings in the area and one of the original sources of accommodation for those taking the waters.

The Pump House, *c.* 1850. This illustration formed one side of a business card produced by Mrs William Sidney Owens, the then proprietor. Bed and board cost £2 2s per week; mineral waters 6d per day; servants board and lodging £1 1s per week and the charge for a 'gentleman introducing a friend to breakfast' was 1s 9d!

The Pump House Hotel and mineral springs, *c.* 1867. By this time extra bedrooms and facilities had been added and rooms including water and chambermaid cost £2 16s a week. The hotel at this time also promised an omnibus service to meet every train.

'Trevonen, in the parish of Cefnllys, County of Radnor on 18th August 1869'. This was described as a 'well known and revered Farm House where many country gentlemen, clergymen and laymen have found sweet repose to recreate their strength and spirits during the past century'.

Stagecoach outside the Rock House Hotel, *c.* 1876. The service between Kington and Llandrindod had been established by Captain Cecil Otway in 1875. A year later he revived the service between Aberystwyth and Presteigne.

The Pump House Hotel in 1879. This photograph depicts the 'old' Pump House as it appeared following extensive additions during the late 1860s and early 1870s. The photograph is inscribed on the reverse by Mr D.D. Morgan, the then proprietor, who died in 1881.

A line engraving, dated July 1880, of Coleman's Hotel and Temple Bazaar, Temple Street. Coleman's Hotel was built in 1872 along with Templefield House and Hampton House. The hotel was later renamed the Bridge Hotel and then the Metropole Hotel.

The Bridge Hotel.

The Metropole Hotel as seen from Beaufort Road. The grand rear facade of the hotel was built in anticipation of the site of the main road through the town being changed.

Llandrindod Wells railway station was first opened in 1865 following completion of the first section of the Central Wales Line between Llandrindod and Knighton. This is one of the most famous views of the town and dates from around 1900 by which time the line was part of the London and North Western Railway Company.

Tom Norton's Cycle Depot, early 1899. It first opened in the Market Hall, High Street in 1898. He was one of the first Raleigh agents in Wales and was himself a pioneer cyclist. In 1949 he was elected President of the Fellowship of Old Time Cyclists; a body whose membership was restricted to those born prior to 1873 who had ridden a pennyfarthing before they were 17.

Charles Jones, blacksmith of Trefonnen Lane with Dorothy and Douglas Jones, outside the Cairn Tea Rooms near the golf course.

The Cottage Hospital and Convalescent Home was first opened in 1880 and was enlarged three years later.

The Midland Bank, Plas Winton Square with a couple of Model T. Fords outside. This site was initially occupied by the North and South Wales Bank Ltd, part of the London City and Midland Bank Ltd.

The Plas Winton Hotel. The building was formerly the rectory of Archdeacon Henry de Winton. The building remains today as the Commodore Hotel. Photograph attributed to Villiers.

Coach and pair outside Middleton House.

The Pump House Hotel and Pump Room around the turn of the century. Built in 1888 by Messrs Shepherd & Sons of Cardiff, it was constructed on the site of the original pump house and farm on which the development of the spa was based. It was requisitioned by the government during the Second World War as an officers' training base and later became a teachers' training college and school for the deaf. Bought in 1973 for Powys County Council, the hotel was demolished in the late 1980s and is now the site of County Hall. Photograph attributed to Villiers.

The new baths and pump house, Pump House Hotel. One of the services offered was a 'hairdressing department'. Part of the building still remains outside County Hall today. Photograph attributed to Villiers.

The Gwalia Hotel on the junction of Ithon Road and Norton Terrace.

'Tom Norton Ltd'. The building was completed in two sections in 1911 and 1919. The site was purchased by Tom Norton at the price of £1 per square yard from Miss J. Sheen, the owner of Plas Winton and other properties in the town. In 1925 the company and site became known as 'The Automobile Palace Ltd'.

'Tom Norton Ltd', prior to 1925. A motor enthusiast, Tom Norton visited the United States in 1912. There he met Henry Ford with whom he carried on a correspondence for some years. Photograph attributed to Roberts.

40

The Rock House Hotel. Photograph attributed to Villiers.

The municipal pump room, Rock Park.

Pump room, Rock Park.

Pump room, Rock Park.

The Grand Pavilion which was built as a concert hall and theatre in 1912. A traditional site for bowling in the town, for a while it too had a pump room for springs discovered during an earlier period of development.

The Ye Wells Hotel. The building, which has become part of Coleg Powys, now stands on the corner of Spa Road East and Beaufort Road. This view shows Spa Road East at a very early stage of development, as yet there is no Beaufort Road to be seen. Photograph attributed to Villiers.

The Town Hall and Old Library.

The Town Hall with the library, now Radnorshire Museum, in the background, illuminated for the coronation of George VI in 1937. The Town Hall was originally known as Brynarlais and was the private residence of Dr W. Bowen Davies, the spa's first resident doctor. It became the Town Hall two years after his death in 1908. The glass conservatory at the back of the building, now the grotto, is just visible.

The Manor Hotel, Lindens Walk.

The Mostyn Hotel, now the Montpellier.

The Court House, built as the County Buildings and Police Station in High Street, photographed prior to its opening in 1909.

Burtons, Provision Merchants, Middleton Street, 1937. It was decorated for both the coronation of George VI and for the *Daily Mail*'s 'Grow and Sell' competition for which there was £5,000 in prize money.

Morris's Imperial Stores and Cafes, the Emporium Buildings. Mr Morris the owner stands outside the shop together with a sign advertising hot luncheons for 2s 3d.

Bird's Cafe, Temple Street.

The Belmont Hotel and Price's Confectioners and Tobacconists.

The new post office, Station Crescent, 1937. This view was taken by A. Selwyn for the official opening.

Four

Religious Life

The Church of St Michael, Cefnllys, 1892.

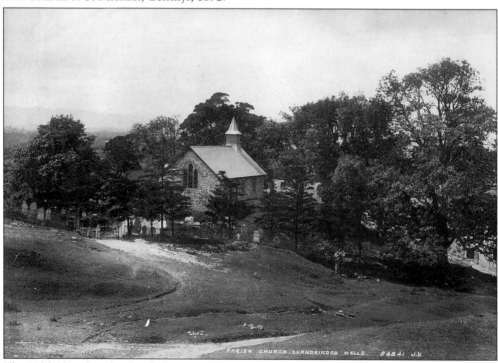

The 'Old Church', Llandrindod Wells. This was the original parish church for Llandrindod and dates from the twelfth century.

Holy Trinity Church, c. 1900. Built as a chapel of ease, it was opened on 26 July 1871 and finally consecrated on 7 September 1882 by which time it could hold 1,400 people. Its construction was funded largely by Messrs Middleton Evans and (later Sir) Richard Green-Price.

WESLEYAN CHURCH, LLANDRINDOD WELLS. 63043 J.V.

The Wesleyan Chapel with the Ye Wells Hotel in the background, c. 1910. The chapel was built in 1905 and closed in the late 1950s. It still stands, unused, today.

The Congregational Chapel on the junction of High Street and Park Crescent in 1904. Built in 1871, it was demolished in the mid-1980s. In the background can be seen the Market Hall, opened in 1872, which was destroyed by a fire in 1957. The poster behind the children

advertises a concert in the Albert Hall by Miss Dina Saul and Mr Meurig James. Down from the Market Hall is Owens', 'Horses and Carriages'.

The Baptist Chapel, Waterloo Road. In 1876 this became the first chapel to be built in the town, the cost being met by public subscription totalling some £900. The chapel has now been demolished.

Llandrindod Church choir leading parishioners from the Church conference held at Llandrindod Wells c. 1910. Among those represented were the Mothers Union and delegations from the parishes of Newbridge, Llandegley, Cascob, Heyope, Llanbadarn Fawr, St Harmon, Llanyre, Nantmel and Glasbury among others. Photograph by Thomas Roberts.

Church conference, *c.* 1910. The large banner towards the back of the procession proclaims: 'The Parishes of Hereford Diocese in Wales Protest Against Dismemberment'. Photograph by Thomas Roberts.

Local officers and committee members of the National Free Church Assembly, 1926. They represented the area in a meeting of the leaders of the Free Church held in the Grand Pavilion. Amongst the local dignitaries present were: Mr Hercules Phillips (Quaker); Rev. Russell Baker (Baptist), Mr Archie Villiers (Congregational), Mr C.C. Hughes (Baptist), Mr T. Hargreaves (Wesleyan Methodist) and Mr Geoffrey Jones (Presbyterian).

Wedding portrait of Matthew Davies and Miss Breeze. Matthew Davies of Chester House, Park Terrace was known as a good carpenter. He later became a funeral director, setting up business behind Barcourt, Temple Street. His wife ran a boarding house in Waterloo Road. Photograph by Rousham Roberts.

Wedding group for the marriage of Francis Hughes to Lance Millward, photographed outside the Brynawel Hotel. The Rev. Russell Baker, the Baptist minister is on the extreme left of the photograph. Photograph by Rousham Roberts.

Five
People

Group of visitors outside the Bridge Hotel, Temple Street, 4 September 1893.

Group of visitors outside the Commercial Union Assurance Company offices, Middleton Street, mid-1890s.

The Hurst family. Originally from Lound, Nottinghamshire, Henry Hurst and his son Joseph were responsible for the construction of many of the early buildings around the Rock Park during the 1860s and 1870s.

An unknown group of visitors to the town. The photograph is inscribed as being 'taken on or about the 28 September 1899 at the Rock House Park, Llandrindod Wells'. Photograph by Villiers.

Visitors relaxing on the common, *c.* 1900.

Coach in Park Terrace, *c.* 1895.

Workers outside the Ye Wells Hotel, 1906.

Willie Roberts, harpist, born 1865. He was one of eight brothers and one sister in the sixth generation of harpists descended from Abram Wood (1699-1799).

Rueben France Roberts, harpist, born 1855. He was the brother of Willie Roberts.

John Roberts, harpist (1816-1894). He was from the fifth generation descended from Abram Wood and the father of Albert, Charlie, Mary Anne, Rueben, Willie, Ernest, John L., Lloyd and James, all of whom played the harp, and who performed several times before Queen Victoria.

John L. Roberts, harpist, born 1853. Photograph by Rousham Roberts.

John L. Roberts preparing to go to a concert.

The staff of 'Tom Norton Ltd', *c.* 1910.

Workers outside the Trefonnen Lane workshop of Charles Jones, blacksmith, *c*. 1910.

The Trefonnen Lane workshop of Charles Jones, blacksmith, *c*. 1910; he hired out horses and carriages.

Tom Norton and J.L. Wilding at the periscope, Llandrindod golf course in 1915. The periscope was built alongside the old sixth tee for golfers to check the fairway ahead was clear.

Charles Jones, blacksmith of Trefonnen Lane, *c*. 1905.

Lakeside Pageant. Photograph by P.B. Abery.

Llandrindod Wells County School, Alexandra Road, 1900s. Photograph by Thomas Roberts.

Llandrindod Wells Council School, Oxford Road, in the early part of this century.

Misses Vaughan Williams' Kincoed private school – 'The Red Caps', outside the Carnegie Free Library, now the Museum, *c.* 1930.

Llandrindod Wells railway station staff. On the far right of the photograph is Alfred Thomas who was station-master here between 1905 and 1945. Photograph by Thomas Roberts.

Llandrindod Wells railway station staff, *c.* 1935.

The Llandrindod Templars, *c*. 1890. Photograph by Thomas Roberts.

The Llandrindod Wells Welsh prize choir who sang before King Edward VII and Queen Alexandra in the Elan Valley on 21 July 1904. Photograph by Thomas Roberts.

71

Children's choir, led by William Thomas, *c.* 1905. Photograph by Thomas Roberts.

Llandrindod wedding, *c.* 1900.

Llandrindod Wells town band in the late 1920s.

The Radnorshire Constabulary. From left to right: Sgt. Goulding, P.C. Albert Williams, P.C. Mickey Morris and P.C. Bert Davies. This was a studio portrait taken by Rousham Roberts.

The Montgomeryshire Yeomanry, Llandrindod Wells station, August 1914. Photograph by Thomas Roberts.

David Lloyd George and his daughter Megan with James Lewis Wilding, Secretary and Director of Llandrindod Wells Golf Club, c. 1920. Both Lloyd George and Neville Chamberlain were regular visitors to the town.

Pony-driven invalid carriage. Photograph by Rousham Roberts.

Beryl Bufton pictured after winning first prize in a fancy dress competition. This was a studio portrait by Rousham Roberts.

Staff of Llandrindod Cottage Hospital. Photograph by Rousham Roberts.

Edna, Gwen and Peggy Eadie. The Eadie family owned a shoe business in High Street before moving to Park Crescent. Studio portrait by Rousham Roberts.

Madame Juliette Paterson dressed as an Arabian princess for a fancy dress competition. Madame Paterson was the French born wife of Col. J. Paterson the County Surveyor for Radnorshire. Studio portrait by Rousham Roberts.

Studio portrait of a family group by Rousham Roberts.

The concierge of the Pump Hotel. Studio portrait by Rousham Roberts.

Francis and Murial Millward, *c.* 1930. Studio portrait by Rousham Roberts.

Miss Thomas, daughter of 'Shakey Thomas' of Shakey Cottage, photographed in Nelson Street with some of her father's hundred plus angora rabbits. Photograph by Rousham Roberts.

Miss Vaughan, photographed just after being evicted from her home 'Castell Dyffryn', Dyffryn Road around 1925. Photograph by Rousham Roberts.

A studio portrait of Miss Swash, by Rousham Roberts, c. 1930.

Poolside at the Metropole Hotel. Photograph by Rousham Roberts.

Unknown mother and daughter, *c.* 1930. Studio portrait by Rousham Roberts.

Studio Portrait by Rousham Roberts of an unidentified brother and sister.

Studio portrait by Rousham Roberts of Miss Probert, *c*. 1930.

A night out at the British Legion, mid-1950s. Photograph by Rousham Roberts.

Relaxing by the poolside at the Metropole Hotel. Photograph by Rousham Roberts.

The staff of W.H. Smith, Coronation, 1953. From left to right: Gerald Mostyn, Miss Jones, Josie Thomas, Mrs George, Mr George (Manager), Enid Davies, Doris Cook, Shirley Swain and Geoff Jones. Photograph by R.G. Sissons.

Six
Sport

The first Llandrindod Wells Football Club which was formed on 1 November 1883.

Llandrindod Wells Football Club, 1894.

Llandrindod Wells Football Club, 1897-8, winners of the South Wales Junior Cup. From left to right, back row: R.E. Moseley, S.G. Williams, A.L. Careless, J.L. Wilding, J. Lane and W.G. Earle. Middle row: J. Arthur, E.J. Sheen, J. Greenwood, W. Bound, P. Jones and G.B. Scandrett. Front row: S.W. Edwards, B. Jones, S. Owens (Captain), H. Morris and H. Davies. Studio portrait by Thomas Roberts.

Llandrindod Wells Football Club, 1898-9, finalists in the Herefordshire Senior Cup. Photograph by Thomas Roberts.

Llandrindod Wells Football Club, 1908-9, winners of the Mid Wales League and Knighton Nurse Challenge Cup. The league at this time consisted of Builth, Brecon Sports, Brecon Depot (South Wales Borderers), Llandrindod Wells, Llanfaes Brigade, Llanwrtyd Wells, Newbridge, Rhayader and Talgarth. Suffering only one defeat in the season, the team was described as 'the best ever seen in the town'. Photograph by Thomas Roberts.

The Ddole Field, *c.* 1870. The photograph depicts a group of polo players although the field was also used as a race course. It later became the site of air displays organised by Tom Norton who tried to develop the area as an airfield.

Llandrindod Wells hockey team, 5 April 1929.

Llandrindod Wells hockey team photographed by Thomas Roberts prior to their match against the Radnorshire Police on the Rock Ground, March 1900. From left to right, back row: Penry Jones; Elysten Bowen Davies; Roger Swettenham; Mr Rees, a local grocer; Mr Dean, an organist; Mr Roberts, one of the family of harpists; W. Wilding. Front row: Mr Pettigrew from Builth Wells; Mr Selwyn; Picton Careless; Mr Lee, a local schoolmaster; Arthur Harper. Photograph by Thomas Roberts.

Llandrindod Wells County Secondary School football team, 1904-5. Photograph by Thomas Roberts.

Llandrindod Wells County School football team. Photograph by Thomas Roberts.

Llandrindod Wells County School football team. Photograph by Thomas Roberts, 1910.

Llandrindod Wells Motorcycle Club outside the Wesleyan Chapel, 31 August 1921. Photograph by R.G. Sissons.

Competitors in a charity football match, 21 March 1923.

Llandrindod Wells Motorcycle Club, 1926.

International Bowling Green, Rock Park. The American Lawn Bowling Team is playing the Mid Wales Bowling Association.

Seven

Events

The rent audit of 20 November 1891, outside the Bridge Hotel.

The laying of the first electric cables in Llandrindod Wells, 1897.

Middleton Street decorated for the coronation of Edward VII, 1901.

The laying of the last turf at the Radnor County Bowling Club, 9 May 1912.

The Swedish aviator, Gustav Hamel who landed on the Rock Park Field on 6 August 1913 (he was lost flying the English Channel in 1915). Hamel's business manager is on the left of the photograph. Whilst in Llandrindod, Hamel is reputed to have flown with a lady passenger holding two piglets to prove that 'pigs could fly'! Photograph by P.B. Abery.

The aviator Vivian Hewitt outside 'Tom Norton Ltd', 6 August 1914. Hewitt flew his Bleriot plane from Rhyl to Phoenix Park, Dublin (with one stopover at Holyhead) in 1 hour 15 minutes. Hewitt was rare amongst the pioneer aviators as a man who survived his passion. He lived in the Bahamas for a while before returning to Britain where he died aged 78 in 1965. Photograph by Thomas Roberts.

Llandrindod Wells Development Association carnival prize winners. Photograph by Rousham Roberts.

David Lloyd George addressing a mass meeting at the Pavilion on the Peace of Versailles. Photograph by P.B. Abery.

The unveiling and dedication of the War Memorial in July 1922. Photograph by P.B. Abery.

The Llandrindod Wells peace choir conducted by Mr Harry Jones which performed at the unveiling ceremony for the War Memorial in July 1922.

Carnival Day 1925. Col. Paterson's 'Gondola' with the Spanish nobleman the Marquis dos Aguas as the gondolier. Photograph by P.B. Abery.

A visit to the town by H.R.H. Edward, Prince of Wales (the future Edward VIII), August 1926. His car is seen passing under the Quarry Road Bridge which was decorated for the occasion.

The Prince of Wales' car passing Selwyn's Newsagent in Park Crescent during the same visit of 1926.

The Prince of Wales taking the waters in the Rock Park, 1926.

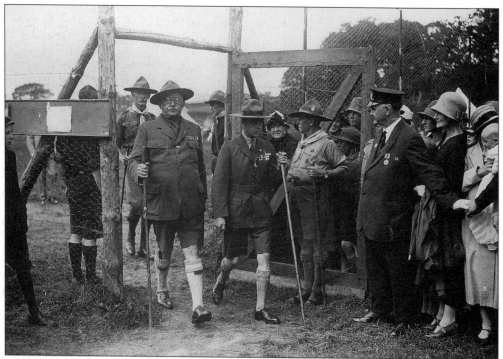

The Prince of Wales on his way to address the crowds during his visit in 1926. Special Constable W.H. Mills can be seen holding back the crowds. Mr Mills was a coal merchant in the town.

The Prince of Wales making presentations to the Scout Jamboree during his visit of 1926.

The recovery of the 'log boat' from the River Ithon by W. F. Grimes of the National Museum of Wales in 1929. Although found close to Castell Collen, the Roman camp, it does come from a later period, probably the eighth or ninth century. Photograph by P.B. Abery.

The recovery of the 'log boat'. Following conservation and study the boat was returned to Llandrindod and presented to the museum. Photograph by P.B. Abery.

The 'log boat' as it appeared after being removed from the river. Photograph by P.B. Abery.

The 'log boat' loaded and ready to be taken away. Photograph by P.B. Abery.

The opening of the pool at the Metropole Hotel.

Llandrindod in mourning for the death of King George V in 1936.

The last air display at Ddole Field, *c*. 1936-37. Photograph by P.B. Abery.

The visit to Llandrindod of Rita Rosslyn who was cycling around the world. Meeting her outside the Town Hall are Rev. Russel Baker, the Baptist minister; Cllr. Seymour Edwards and Hercules Phillips, newspaper reporter. Photograph by Rousham Roberts.

Restocking the River Ithon with fish. Photograph by Rousham Roberts.

Crowds waiting for the arrival of the competitors in the 1938 International Motorcycle Trials. Photograph by Rousham Roberts.

Opposite: The starting point of the 1938 International Motorcycle Trials. Of note is the Swastika representing the German team. This is reputedly one of the very few occasions that the Nazi flag was flown in Britain. Photograph by Rousham Roberts.

The bandstand decorated for the 1938 International Motorcycle Trials. Photograph by Rousham Roberts.

Competitors at the International Six Day Trial of 1938. Photograph by Rousham Roberts.

Middleton Street, 6 March 1947, following the 'Great Blizzard'.

Middleton Street, 6 March 1947.

Gwalia Square, with Lindens Hotel and Holy Trinity Church in the background.

Temple Street, 6 March 1947.

Carnival day, Llandrindod Wells, late 1930s. Photograph by C. Selwyn.

Llandrindod railway station dressed for the royal visit of Queen Elizabeth II and Prince Philip, 23 October 1952.

Queen Elizabeth II and Prince Philip leaving Llandrindod Wells station, 23 October 1952.

Mr Lloyd carving the commemorative stone to mark the spot where Queen Elizabeth II first set foot in Wales following her accession to the throne. The stone came from the Claerwen Dam. Photograph by A. H. Selwyn.

Laying the commemorative stone, Llandrindod Wells Station, 1952. Photograph by R.G. Sissons.

Carnival queen and attendants, Llandrindod Wells, c. 1950. Included in the photograph are Maud Brickley, Janet Hines, Jean Davies, Maureen Brookes and Kay Maddox, the Carnival queen. Photograph attributed to Percy Roberts.

Eight
Newbridge-on-Wye

The Old Baptist Chapel, Newbridge-on-Wye, 1864.

The Newbridge Horse Fair, *c.* 1905.

The Newbridge Horse Fair, 1927.

The Powell family leaving Brochen Farm, Newbridge to live in Wem. Photograph by P.B. Abery.

The parish church, Newbridge-on-Wye.

The interior of the parish church, Newbridge-on-Wye, 1883.

Newbridge-on-Wye, with, on the left, the Sun Inn.

School and Memorial Fountain.   *Newbridge-on-Wye.*

The school and the memorial fountain, Newbridge-on-Wye. The fountain commemorates the first vicar of All Saints, the Rev. John Edward Lloyd.

The bridge over the Wye, Newbridge-on-Wye.

Llysdinam Hall, Newbridge-on-Wye.

'A Sylvan Scene', Newbridge-on-Wye.

Commemorative banners celebrating the marriage of Sir Charles Llewellyn and Agnes Minna Venables of Llysdinam, 23 August 1893.

The building of the new bridge over the Wye.

Testing the strength of the new bridge over the Wye by driving a steam engine over it, 1911.

The Rev. J.E. Lloyd and family photographed at the vicarage in 1883.

Outside Bryn yr Drodded, Llysdinam. Note the old cheese press on the left of the picture.

Hope's Stores, general merchants, *c*. 1917.

Newbridge Carnival, mid-1920s. Photograph by P.B. Abery.

130

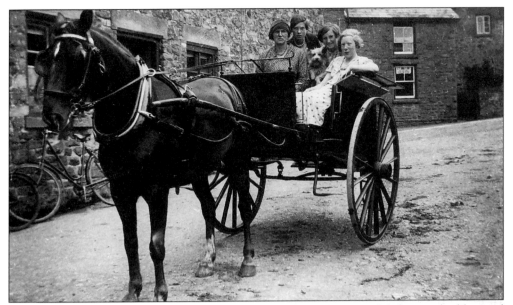

Mrs Hope with family. As well as being general merchants the Hope family were builders and undertakers.

Mr Evan Ambrose Ebenezer Jones Powell outside All Saints, Newbridge, 1898.

Church choir, 1897.

Newbridge Amateur Dramatic Society at the reading room.

Ladies' Church conference.

The opening of the new bridge over the Wye. The photograph is captioned: 'Llysdinam Bridge, Newbridge-on-Wye being opened by Mr and Mrs Venables Llewellyn's infant son of Llysdinam Hall March 29th 1911'.

Newbridge football team, 23 March 1901.

One of the first premium bond prize draw tickets bought in Newbridge post office. It was sold by Mrs Pritchard the postmistress to Tom Pugh the postman, 11 June 1957.

Newbridge Football Club, 1907/8 season.

The Girls Friendly Society, Newbridge-on-Wye, 1911 annual outing.

Harry Alford with one of the family's vans.

William Powell, one of Alford's drivers.

Senior class at Newbridge-on-Wye Primary School, *c.* 1897.

A late nineteenth century view of the new Baptist Chapel.

Alford's Stores and the Cambrian Steam Bakery. In its heyday this was one of the biggest bakeries in the area.

The road to Rhayader pictured on New Year's Day 1901.

Newbridge-on-Wye. In the left foreground is the Bell's Shop which was demolished in 1912.

The village of Newbridge-on-Wye, looking south, 1904.

The post office, *c*. 1920.

The first post office – 'Brooklyn' – in Newbridge with (second from the left) Mrs Annie Powell, the first postmistress. Also picture are Mary Alice Lloyd and Mrs Price, who would become postmistress at the new post office, 'Earlsmead'.

Newbridge-on-Wye station, 1956. The last train came through in December 1962.

Newbridge-on-Wye railway station looking north. The station closed in 1963 as a result of the Beeching Axe which dramatically cut the number of lines in operation in Wales and the rest of the United Kingdom.

Newbridge-on-Wye station, 1911.

Newbridge Horse Fair, one of the biggest in the country, shortly after the First World War.

The Upper Shop, c. 1902, with Mr David Evans the butcher and his cart.

Crown Row, 1920s.

The Meredith Family, constructors of many of the buildings in Llandrindod Wells and Llanidloes. From left to right, back row: Robert, Edward, Alfred, Henry and Daniel. Front row: Agnes, Margaret, Hannah, May and Rachel.

Those men from Newbridge and district who fought in, and returned from, the 1914-18 war. Although the photograph was taken in 1919 some of the men had still not returned from active service.

Tenants of Doldowlod Estate outside the Rock Park Hotel, 1910

The 'Old Bridge' over the Wye with Arthur Griffiths, standing and William Evans, 1908.

Nine
Around Llandrindod

The Bridge, Howey.

St David's Church, Howey.

150

The post office, Howey.

Howey.

The Mill, Howey.

Howey Choir, the winners of the Kingsland Silver Challenge Cup in 1911 and 1912. Studio portrait by Rousham Roberts.

An automobile accident at Howey Bridge, 23 September 1912. Photograph by Thomas Roberts.

Pony-driven invalid carriage run by Tommy Hamer of Howey. Photograph by Rousham Roberts.

Hadley and Evan Matthews who ran the grocer's and baker's in Howey.

Baptisms in Howey Brook. The brook was specially dammed during the 1950s for baptisms.

Parish church of St Cewydd, Disserth. This church on the road between Newbridge-on-Wye and Howey dates from the thirteenth century.

Llanyre Bridge.

The first 'Congregation of the Quaker Chapel' near Deuarth, Llanyre, July 1894.

Crossgates Juniors football team, photographed by Percy Roberts in the early 1950s.

The Aberystwyth to Presteigne stage outside the Severn Arms, Penybont around 1880. The coach service was revived in 1876 by Captain Otway.

Crowds outside the Severn Arms, Penybont, *c.* 1904. The posters on the wall advertise Buffalo Bill's Wild West Show which toured the country in the early years of the century.

The Penybont Show, *c.* 1904.

Tom Price Senior, blacksmith of Penybont.

Hammond's of Penybont removal van.

The Pales Meeting House, Penybont. This was built in 1717 next to the Quaker graveyard which had been acquired in 1673. Its remoteness is a testament to early persecution. The Quakers used part of the building as a school from 1867.

Penybont football team as photographed by Percy Roberts in the early 1950s.

The local hunt outside the Severn Arms, Penybont, *c.* 1950. Photograph by Percy Roberts.